IMAGES OF ENGLAND

AROUND
REDCAR

IMAGES OF ENGLAND

AROUND
REDCAR

SHEILA BARKER

TEMPUS

Frontispiece: Dorman Long Warrenby Athletic Club annual outing, *c.* 1940. Included in the photograph are: Mrs Wheeler and daughters Margaret, Martha and Mary; Grandma Lloyd, Mrs Lloyd, Jim and Freda Lloyd; Mr Bishop; Mrs Oliver with Betty and Mary; Mrs Spence with Dulcia and Ivy; Mrs Phillips and Dick; Mrs Leath, Brenda Maltby; Mr and Mrs Readman with Paul, Sheila, Keith and Olga Readman; Iris Sorrell and her sister, Lucy Harrington.

First published 2005

Tempus Publishing Limited
The Mill, Brimscombe Port,
Stroud, Gloucestershire, GL5 2QG
www.tempus-publishing.com

British Library Cataloguing in Publication Data.
A catalogue record for this book is available from the British Library.

ISBN 0 7524 3704 6

Typesetting and origination by Tempus Publishing Limited.
Printed in Great Britain.

Contents

Acknowledgements

Thank you to everyone who has helped in any way with the compilation of this book.

My gratitude goes to Jim White, Sue Barker, Linda Maude, John O'Neil, my husband Colin and our family, for their encouragement and support over these past months.

To the following people who contributed photographs, and information: Ian and Glenda Hall, Alan and Mavis Waller, Jenny Kellet, Merle Hill, Wendy Hall, Norma Wilson, Freda Anderson, Sheila Bracken, George Ireland, Brenda Oliver Jarret, David Armstrong, Keith Burn and members of the Redcar Male Voice Choir, Roy and Davina Barker, Rose Morrison, Elaine Alexander, Arthur and Pauline Blower, Dennis Wardle, Evelyn Walker and Keith Milburn, John Banks and 'The United Enthusiasts', George Ayton, Marlene Calvert, Violet Bullock, Allan Temke, Mr Gladwin, Tony and Peggy Farrer, Doreen Wright, Bill and Tricia Bradley, Ann Knight, Judith Graham, Margaret Thompson, Margaret Powlay, Peggy Westbrook, Margaret Jordan, Ann Ivison, Jean Wood, Ken Thompson, Maureen Bousher, Kathleen Minnery, Maurice Nunn, Allison Small, Bill and Margaret Troup, Bruce Ross, Jim Thompson MBE, Ron Sabison BEM, Sylvia Carling, Kathleen Lambert and the Gibbon family, John Partridge (Redcar Town Manager), Redcar Cricket Club, E. Ransom (Honorary Curator of the Zetland Lifeboat museum) and the *Evening Gazette*.

Thank you to everyone who contributed photographs to my website 'The Marsh' (www.communigate.co.uk/ne/themarsh).

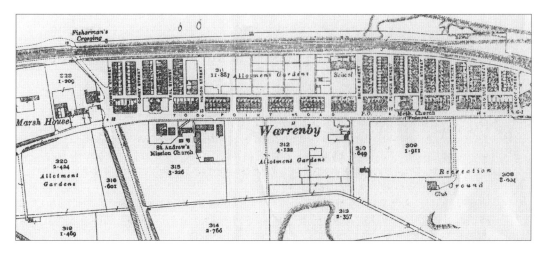

Introduction

Redcar is a seaside town on the north-east coast of England. Early records tell us that Redcar and Coatham were two small fishing ports in the North Riding of Yorkshire.

In 1808 William Hutton of Birmingham, who at the age of eighty-five started upon a journey to the remote part of Yorkshire accompanied by his daughter and a servant, arrived in the area. Mr Hutton said, 'After travelling 184 miles we arrived at Coatham and Redcar, which although two villages, or rather hamlets, are in the infancy of their existence. Coatham is only half a street that is built only on one side about 400 yards long, and consists of about seventy houses. We then pass over an open space of 400 yards more which brings us to Redcar, which is one street built 500 yards long containing about 160 houses.' Hutton's visit took place forty-four years before Mrs Theresa Newcomen laid the foundation stone of Christ Church, Coatham.

Fishing and farming were the main factors of the economy, but Redcar adjusted well to the new industrial age. In the mid-1800s Redcar took advantage of the extension of the Stockton & Darlington Railway line and entered into the iron trade.

Warrenby village came into being during the 1870s, when homes were erected by Messrs Robson, Maynard & Co. to house the immigrant ironworkers and their families who arrived from all over the British Isles. The new village was named Warrentown, and later renamed Warrenby. In 1917 Dormanstown was built to house the families of the increasing number of steelworkers coming to the area and being employed by Dorman Long.

The history of Redcar has been well established by several writers of local history. The purpose of this book is to gather a representative selection of photographs taken through the ages, which give an insight into the life and times of the people who lived in the communities around Redcar.

Being closely connected by strong neighbourly ties, much shared activity and lasting relationships, these communities shared a social history that passed through periods of great change, with every decade leaving a legacy of memories.

Many will remember the views of Redcar presented here, and may recall the changes that have been made to roadways and buildings over the years. For people new to the area, or those too young to remember, they will provide a fascinating insight into Redcar of another time.

I sincerely hope you enjoy this collection of pictures drawn from personal photograph albums and copies of preserved archive material, which collectively offer a nostalgic glimpse into times past.

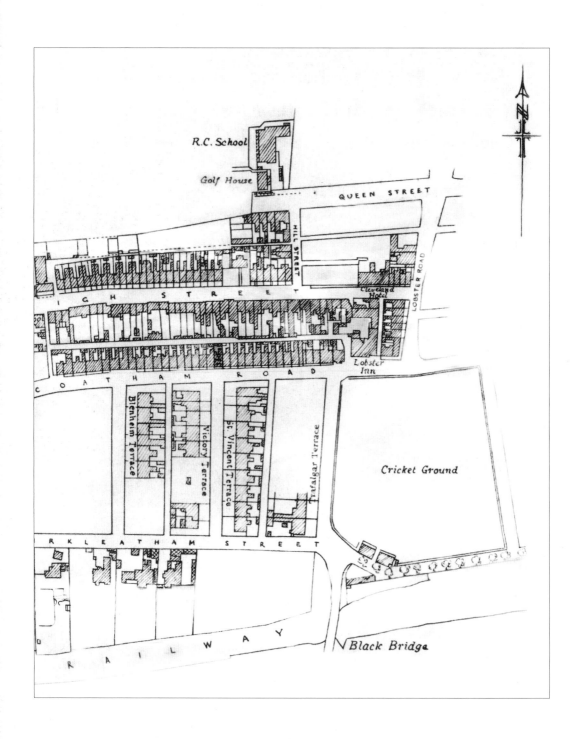

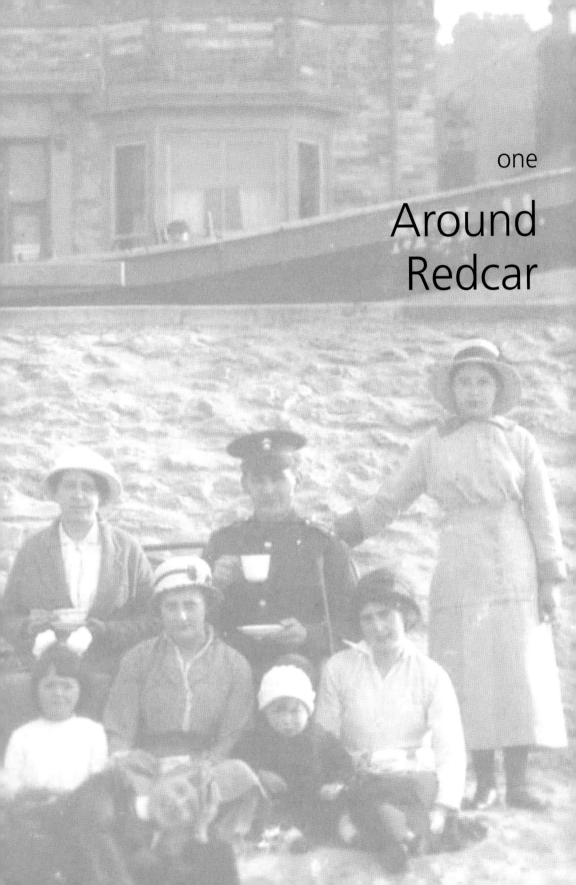

one

Around Redcar

CLOCK TOWER AND HIGH STREET, REDCAR.

E Gordon Scott they called him,
A man of some renown.

He made the ship that sails up there,
Above old Redcar Town.

Twas in his Lord Street Smithy
Where it was planned and wrought,
and with him worked a young lad
apprentice whom he taught.

When I am in the High Street
I look bove the clock,
and gratefully remember
My father and his shop.

I gaze up there and wonder
how many people know
Who made the ship that sails up there,
So many years ago.?

By Kathleen Gordon Rusk

Above: The King Edward VII Memorial Clock is a Grade II-listed building featured against a backdrop looking right to West Terrace and the Central Cinema. On the left of the High Street is the famous sign of Amos Hinton who owned a chain of grocery shops throughout the north of England. Hinton's were renowned for the quality of their own brand-named products.

Left: A poem written by Kathleen Gordon Rusk as a tribute to her father, providing the fascinating history of the sailing ship weather vane.

The first Marquis of Zetland, pictured in 1910.

South Terrace, *c.* 1800.

Left: Local dignitary William Baker, whose obituary was as follows: 'The death occurred this morning 21 October 1910 of Mr Wm Baker, of High Street Redcar, a well known tradesman in the seaside town. The deceased, who was sixty-two years old, took a keen interest in Municipal affairs, and for nearly twenty years served on the local Sanitary Authority. He was also an overseer for Redcar. A few years ago he occupied the position of chairman of the Urban Council.'

Below: A picture postcard featuring the historical demolition of the last cruck house in Redcar.

High Street Redcar, *c.* 1918.

The Promenade, *c.* 1918.

St Peter's Church, Redcar, *c.* 1909.

Above: The interior of St Peter's Church, *c.* 1917.

Opposite below: The society wedding during 1908 of Anna Wilkinson of Redcar and Harry Kelsey, a Scarborough Chemist, pictured in the grounds of the Grange. Back row, extreme left: Isaac Wilkinson (the bride's brother). Front row, seated second left: Emily Caroline Wilkinson (the bride's sister).

Above: The Grange, pictured here around 1900, was the family home of the Wilkinson family. The house, which was situated in Easson Road, stood in 1½ acres of land and was taken over during the war years to house troops. Eventually the property was sold by auction at the Swan Hotel, Redcar. A bid for £3,000 from a local doctor was refused, and the house was sold to another bidder for an undisclosed sum.

The *Zetland* lifeboat, which is kept at the Zetland Museum at Redcar, has been added to the National Historic Ships core collection. The *Zetland* was the eleventh lifeboat to be built by Henry Greathead of South Shields at a cost of £200. She is the only surviving lifeboat out of a total of thirty-one that he built, and is the oldest lifeboat in the world.

Arriving at Redcar on 6 October 1802, the *Zetland* has celebrated her bicentenary. She served Redcar and passing seafarers from 1802 until 1880, and is credited with saving over 500 lives. *Zetland* was the forerunner of today's RNLI. Housed on the seafront at Redcar where her life's work was so courageously performed, the *Zetland* takes pride of place in Redcar's history. The treacherous north-east coast needed a reliable boat for stormy weather, and welcomed the arrival of the *Zetland*. Although Redcar was only a small village, there was never a shortage of volunteers to man her.

Above and below: The funeral of Mr Thomas Hood Picknett, which took place in 1935, included the last horse-drawn cortege to leave Redcar. This was a fitting tribute, since Mr Picknett was the last surviving member of the old *Zetland* lifeboat crew.

Above: Redcar beach, *c.* 1917. Nellie Ramsdale is the young lady standing beside the table wearing a pinny. Nellie was working in service for a family who lived on Coatham Road. The young lady standing to the far right is Nellie's younger sister Alice.

Left: Nellie and Alice Ramsdale on Redcar beach, *c.* 1917.

Farmer Tom Hill working his land at Wheatlands Farm, Redcar, *c.* 1930.

Thrashing day at Wheatlands Farm in the 1930s.

Above: Porteous' Fish and Chips Saloon, Dundas Street, *c.* 1935. From left to right: –?–, –?–, –?–, Mabel Porteous, Will Porteous, –?–, –?–, –?–.

Left: Mabel Porteous in High Street, Redcar.

Porteous' Fish and Chips Saloon during the Second World War, providing commodities for local people and day-trippers during a period of food rationing.

Will and Mabel Porteous out walking in High Street, Redcar.

The Swan Hotel and Roebucks department store in the 1940s.

High Street, Redcar. Prominent is the National Provincial Bank of England, Tyler's Shoe Shop and Murdoch's London Warehouse.

From left to right: Norma Wilson, June Pinkney, Olive Porter, (?) manager of the local cinema, June Patterson, Pam Easson, Ann Brownbridge. The girls were modelling swimsuits for Teasdale's, a local seafront store, *c.* 1949.

The Red Lion Hotel on High Street, *c.* 1925.

Above: High Street in the 1930s. Prominent is the Queen's Hotel.

Left: The sign, from 1935, reads 'New ballroom now open'. The ballroom was taken over as sleeping quarters for the RAF during the Second World War.

Opposite above: Landlord and landlady Jim and Jenny Kellet at the Queen's Hotel, *c.* 1955.

Opposite below: The ballroom at the Queen's.

Above: Her Majesty Queen Elizabeth visiting the area in 1956.

Left: Annie Martin and her daughter Davina alighting a United Bus in Redcar High Street.

Opposite above: The No. 64 United Bus waiting on Platform 3 in Redcar Bus Station. St Peter's Church can be seen in the background.

Opposite below: The No. 285 bus on Kirkleatham Lane, destination Green Lane, on 6 August 1969. *(Photograph courtesy of John Banks)*

Long-serving Redcar milkman Ben
Ayton on his rounds.

Harold Kelsey, proprietor of Kelsey's
radio and cycle shop on Station
Road.

Picknett's Wet Fish Shop, Queen Street. In the doorway is Tom Picknett with his daughter Grace. On the left: Laurie Picknett, Beryl ?, Dennis Preston.

A well-known feature of the 1960s, The Deep Sea Beatles, on show in Picknett's fish shop window.

Above: On the left in cricket whites is young Allan Temke pictured near his home in Albert Street with his cousin Patrick on the right and friend Alan Waugh of Lord Street in the centre.

Left: Rose and Carl Temke of 2 Albert Street.

Opposite below: In the back alley of 2 Albert Street, Barbara Lister with her daughter Susan.

Above: Alma Parade outside the home of Amelia Robinson. A large group of family and friends gather to celebrate the sixteenth birthday of Arthur Robinson, pictured in uniform and standing behind his grandmother Eliza Temke. Front row, right: Rose Temke. Back row, second left: Rose's husband, Carl Temke. Amelia occupied the house, which was originally the first police station in Redcar.

Blower's paint and wallpaper store, at the junction of Lord Street and Redcar Lane.

The proprietor Mr Blower and his assistant in the Redcar Lane shop. Mr Blower went on to open a second shop on Redcar High Street around 1970.

Gladwin's carpets, established in 1946.

Staff from the Maypole grocer's shop, *c.* 1960. Descending: Rita Rudland Susan Stout, Linda Close.

From left to right: the manager of Esso, Linda Close, Mrs Hand, Pat Arbon, Ray Buckwell, Mr Hand, Jim Callaghan, -?-. Mr and Mrs Hand were receiving the keys to a car on behalf of their son who was serving in the navy. The car was a raffle prize which had been donated by Esso to a local charity.

Above and right: Carol and Gillian Wood
exploring in Locke Park during the 1960s.

CHILDRENS BOATING POOL, REDCAR.   83799

The children's boating pool, *c.* 1925.

Colonel Locke, a surgeon, bequeathed £5,000 to be used to purchase land for the benefit of the people of Redcar. As a consequence Locke Park was opened in 1930. Depicted here is the boathouse viewed from the island.

Left: Hephzibah Blower holding son Arthur, with William in a sailor suit, Dora at the rear and Effie at the side.

Below: Christening day, *c.* 1960. From left to right: Violet Wise, Doris Blower, Elizabeth Caddy, baby Susan Anne Blower, and Pauline Blower.

When this book is open,
When on this page you frown,
Think of the one who spoilt it,
By writing upside down.

Jack Robinson 1920.
22ND JANUARY

Gather your rosebuds while you may
Old time is still a flying.
And the Same sweet flower
            that blooms today.
Tomorrow may be dying.

Annie Heugh.
26. 10. 23.

We are atoms which float on the river of years,
    On our way to an ultimate sea;
And time with its swiftness, its joys; and its tears,
    Brings its changes to you and to me.
But if as swift-footed years hurry by,
    We lose sight of each other at last;
Let us ever remember that we – you and I
    Were once friends in the far-reaching past.

A.P. Siddle
Sept 2nd 1919

Autographs from a private inherited collection.

ROTARY CLUB OF REDCAR

20th ANNUAL
DONKEY DERBY

Redcar Racecourse

SUNDAY, 1st JULY 1990

Admission:
Adults 50p Children FREE

Sponsored by

HORNCASTLE
MOTOR COMPANY LTD.

Left: A poster advertising a Rotary Club charity event in 1990.

Below: Guests of the Rotary Club at the Donkey Derby. From left to right: -?-, -?-, Mrs M. Waller, Mo Mowlam (MP for Redcar) , -?-, -?-, -?-.

Redcar Rotary Club members. From left to right, front row: Vin Keegan, -?-, Charles Appleyard, Ron Hall, Jim Macrae, Danny Horton. Middle row: John Fellows, Eric Whitehead, John Little, Jack Bower, Bill Campbell, Les Hansell, Tom Ridley, Ken Mawson, Jim Robertson, Alan Brundall, Alan Waller, Jim Croskell. Top left: Ken Wetherell.

Members of Redcar Buffs Club, 1971.

Redcar and Coatham Cricket Club, early members, *c.* 1910.

Redcar Cricket Club, First XI, 1956.

The Redcar Crusaders football team celebrate at a presentation evening. Don Bullock is in the centre of the middle row.

Sacred Heart senior football team. From left to right, back row: Peter McCarthy, Tony Skidmore, Les Ord, Nobby Hobson, Terry White, John Hall. Front row: Frankie Harker, Ted Riley, Jimmy Sullivan, Brian O'Hara, Jimmy Emmerson.

Above: Redcar Pier. Linda Close is sitting in the foreground.

Right: The Fiddler family, 474 miles from home, *c.* 1960.

Opposite above: Dormanstown Junior School hall, in the 1960s. The pupils are being cared for by their teachers: on the left Miss Rudkin and Mrs Banks and on the right Headmaster Mr Price.

Opposite below: Coatham County Modern hockey team, *c.* 1972. From left to right, back row: Janet ?, Alison Screenan, Linda Carol, Sharon Adams, Susan Lister. Middle row: Denise Sheriff, Jillian Calvert, Susan Addison, Lesley Patterson. Front row: Diane ?, Angela McLaughlan, Kim Johnson, Susan Caffrey, Diane ?

Left: Redcar postman Tony Farrer making a very special delivery to Marina Avenue.

Below: German prisoners of war after a day working on Wheatlands Farm.

two

Coatham

Above: Christ Church, Coatham, was built in 1854 and was known as the 'church-in-the-fields'. It was said at that time to be the most beautiful church in Cleveland.

Left: Wilf Thurwell escorts his daughter Doreen to her wedding at Christ Church, 1951.

Above: Church House, the parish community centre.

Right: Buckenham's butchers on Coatham Road, established in the early 1900s.

The Municipal Buildings and Cenotaph, Coatham Road.

The Coatham Convalescent Home was built in 1860, during the jurisdiction of the Revd John Postlethwaite, the first Vicar of Coatham.

Opposite above: George Thurwell walking on Coatham Road, *c.* 1930.

Opposite below: The Thurwell Family – Wilf, his wife Florence and their children Sonny and Doreen – captured on Coatham Sands, *c.* 1928.

Above: Many families spent happy holidays at Barker's Holiday Camp on Warrenby Road. There were chalets and caravans for hire and the holidaymakers were catered for with a shop and a fried fish shop on site, and two general dealers nearby. The families regularly met up for holidays, many coming from the mining communities of Durham.

Dennis Wardle's late parents, Doris and Billy Hunter, owned a hut on the campsite beside the Saltburn to Darlington railway line on Barker's field, which meant being awakened by the first train every morning at around 5.00 a.m. Dennis remembers meeting a family from Boston arriving at the gate looking bemused, as if they thought they had arrived at a prisoner of war camp!

There was a corrugated iron dwelling named Suitsus, a name that stuck in his memory, and also a gypsy's caravan for hire, and at tea-time each day an old boy came around selling paraffin.

Left: L.H. Barker, the popular Mayor of Redcar, 1966.

The interior of the new Sacred Heart Church on Lobster Road, *c.* 1920.

The clergy at the Sacred Heart presbytery, July 1963. From left to right: Father Manley, Monsignor Brunner, Father Ryan.

The Barkers from Marina Avenue on Coatham Sands, 1963. From left to right: Maureen, Ann, Paul, Colin.

Right: Maureen Barker leaving her Marina Avenue home on a winter's morning. The snow is defining the rooftops on Rocket Terrace.

Opposite above: Coatham Pier, 1875.

Opposite below: Children playing in Rocket Terrace, 1965. Rocket Terrace had been the original headquarters of the Rocket Brigade. Many lives at sea were saved by means of shooting a line, by rocket apparatus on a tripod, to ships in distress offshore.

Above left: On the right is David Martin in full dress uniform, *c.* 1929.

Above right: Annie Martin (on the right) with her Red Cross colleague in 1925.

Opposite above: Pierson Street fire brigade, *c.* 1939. On the left is Mr Outhwaite with his young son Barry.

Opposite below: The Red Cross ambulance service. From left to right: -?-, David Martin, -?-, W. Clarke.

White House School primary class, 1949. Second from the left, back row: Mildred Wild. Second from the right, back row: Wendy Fiddler. Both girls lived on Coatham Road.

The Gables was formerly Coatham Vicarage. In the 1950s the premises became a residential home for the elderly. Here enjoying themselves on a trip to Blackpool are members of staff from the nursing home. From left to right: Winnie and Harry Graham, Winnie Gibbon, Freda Wilson, Mrs Thwaites, and the matron of the Gables.

Redcar British Legion founder members, c. 1950. From left to right, top row: Jack Reveley (Second World War), Dougie Mackay (Second World War), William Carter (Boer War), Charles Warrington (First World War), Charles Berry (Second World War), William Claughey (Second World War). Bottom row: Samuel Bull (Boer War), Thomas Snowdon (Boer War).

A social evening at the Cleveland Hotel, 1959. From left to right seated: -?-, Dolly Turner, --?-, -?-, Fred Lister, Betty Lister, Julien Lister. Standing: -?-, Jack Turner, -?-.

Left: A snapshot taken while walking on Redcar Promenade. From left to right: Alison Morgan, Mrs Craggs, -?-.

Below: 'Our Gang' is written on the back of this 1930s photograph. From left to right: Dorothy Leng, Doreen Thurwell, Edna Johnston, May Sturman, Muriel Johnston, Ida Wilson,? Robertson.

Stead Memorial Hospital, Kirkleatham Street, Coatham, 1940.

Christmas morning at Stead Memorial Hospital. On the right in the front row is Nurse Peggy Westbrook.

Above left: Mr and Mrs James Emmerson married in 1934 and enjoyed seventy happy years of married life.

Above right: Harrington House, 1930.

Opposite above: Pope John Paul II welcomes Father Cush and Miss Durkin to Rome along with other members of the Sacred Heart Parish in April 1984.

Opposite below: Junior members at the golf club, 1908.

Sacred Heart School class photograph, c. 1947. From left to right, back row: Colin Gibbon, Laurie Rea, John Smith, Tony Hamill, Tommy Kelly, Peter Broome, Maurice Barker. Middle row: Colin Barker, Peter Hudson, Kenneth Moran, Maureen McCormick, Patricia Skelton, Doreen Guy, -?-, John Hall, Terry Colvin. Front row: Charlotte McMormick, Mary O'Grady, Theresa Kelly, -?-, Maria Organ, Mr C. Mullarky, Mary Matthews, -?-, Mary Sandel, -?-, Kathleen Faulkner.

Mr Arthur Nash and partner Mr Gerald Fleming were founders of the Redwing Bus Co. in Redcar. *(Photograph courtesy John Banks Collections)*

Above: A group of people off for a day trip leaving Coatham High Street, *c.* 1950. Included in the picture are Mrs Gerard, Mrs Dawkins, Miss Moir, Mrs Nash, Mr Roberts, Mrs Pierson and Mr Linford.

Opposite below: In front of Sacred Heart Church, 1989. From left to right: Steve Knight, Colin Barker, Sheila Barker, Ann Knight.

The 287 United bus travelling from Warrenby Village to New Marske, pictured on Coatham Road.

Wilf Thurwell (on the right) enjoying a day out with Coatham pensioners, 1965.

Tommy Lightfoot at Redcar's open-air swimming pool at Coatham enclosure, *c.* 1935.

Leith Johnson and Dorothea Sexton (*née* Johnson) during the 1920s at the Coatham enclosure.

Above: The National Registration card of Charles Fiddler of Coatham Road.

Left: The staff of the Gables including Winnie Gibbon, Freda Wilson, and Vi Whitham.

Opposite above: Benbows Chemist, Coatham Road, *c.* 1950. Sheila Caddy (on the right) is taking a breath of sea air with her work colleague.

Opposite below: Whilst visiting Redcar in his capacity as an MP, Enoch Powell paid a visit to the York Hotel on Coatham Road to meet Mrs Flo Maher the organizer of a popular ladies' luncheon club.

Members of Redcar Boys' Brigade.

Above left: Robert Powlay practising his reveille on Barker's fields a fair distance from his home.

Above right: Robert and Brian Powlay following in father's footsteps, *c.* 1940.

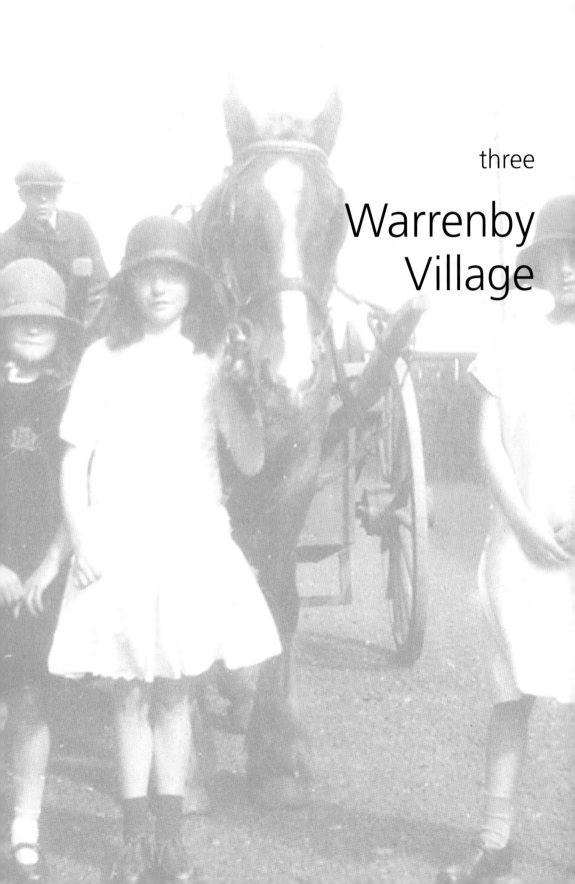

three

Warrenby
Village

Tod Point Road, Warrenby.

Around nine o'clock on the evening of Friday 14 June 1895, the few Warrenby people who were out of doors heard an unusually loud noise at the furnaces of Walker, Maynard & Co. Then they saw a great deal of dust, water and steam rise high into the air and an immense glare light the sky with exceptional brilliance. Those who ran to the works to investigate found that the explosion had been far worse than they imagined. The actual cause was not immediately known but it did appear that a boiler, one of fifteen, some of which were 60ft in length, had burst, causing the others to burst in quick succession. However, whatever the reason, eleven of the boilers had been destroyed and debris from them and brickwork and buildings had been carried over a distance of several hundred yards. At the sound of the explosion doctors and priests were sent for and there was a desperate rush to find and tend to the injured. While minor wounds had been inflicted on workmen some distance from the centre of the explosion, some of those who were near had sustained frightful injuries due mainly to the effect of scalding steam. When one man was found, for example, some of the rescuers fainted, so disfigured was his body. Some of the injured struggled or were carried to their homes and a number were taken by train to the Cottage Hospital, North Ormesby. Among those conveyed to the hospital were: John Kelly and Michael Turner, both of 5 Widgeon Street, James Murphy of 14 Partridge Street, Patrick Husson of Widgeon Street and Michael Carnegie. Other known injured were Thomas Lickiss, Joseph Lickiss, J.W. Wetherill, Thomas Taylor, Daniel Dooley, George Fresson and Michael Carnegie.

Opposite above: Tod Point Road, Warrenby Village, *c.* 1800.

Opposite below: A group of early Warrenby settlers. George William Ayton is second right in the back row.

For those who had been thrown out of work because of the explosion, much depended on whether they were members of one of the numerous friendly or benefit societies which, on payment of a small weekly sum, entitled them to draw a fixed amount each week. However, the amounts involved were usually only sufficient to tide them over until work was resumed. Thus many of the Warrenby families were in financial difficulties, though some workmen did gain temporary employment with other firms. A similar situation faced the widows and orphans and the families of the injured, and it was the recognition of the inadequacy of provision, even when the men had been insured, that prompted the starting of a Relief Fund under the chairmanship of the Mayor of Middlesbrough, with a central and a local committee.

Funds were raised through the performances of such groups as the Apollo Male Voice Choir, the proceeds of cycle racing at the Grangetown track, and the demonstrations of friendly societies in the local towns. Along with prominent people such as the local Member of Parliament and the Bishop of Middlesbrough making donations, and collections being made at the local works, the fund gradually grew, and after two weeks the local committee recommended that temporary relief should be granted on the following basis:

2s 6d (12½p) to widows
1s 6d (7½p) to each child under ten years
2s (10p) to each child over ten years and under fourteen years

The families of the injured were assisted on the same scale. Injured men not in hospital were to receive the same as widows.

The McCarthy family mourn the loss of a husband and father, Patrick Peter McCarthy, who lost his life in the Warrenby disaster. Barbara is standing near her mother, Patrick Peter is sitting on the left, Jim in his mother's arms, and John is sitting at the front. Nora and her children were all suitably dressed in customary black; their mother had explained to the children that this was a mark of respect for their beloved father.

Sacred To The Memory Of,

PATRICK MOORE, JOHN GALE, EDWARD AYTON,
PATRICK M'CARTHY, JAMES HALLIGAN,
GEORGE WALLACE, HENRY BARKER, ROBERT WRAY
AND EDWARD DOOLEY.

Who Lost Their Lives, in the Terrible BOILER EXPLOSION
AT WARRENBY IRONWORKS, NEAR REDCAR.
JUNE, 14TH. 1895.

Take warning by our sudden call, · For in our lives we little thought
That you for death prepare, Our end had been so near,
For it will come, you know not when, All you that have a longer time,
The manner, how, or where. For death Oh! then prepare.

The explosion killed four men and seriously injured nineteen others, of whom eight later died: Harry Baker (37) a boilerman of Coney Street, married with two children; Peter Moore (27) a mine filler of Plover Street, married with one child; John Gale (21) a mine filler of Warrenby, married with two children; Patrick Peter McCarthy (38) a charger of Widgeon Street, married with four children; James Halligan (28) a mine filler of James Terrace; George Wallace (30) a blast-furnaceman of James Terrace; Edward Ayton (24) a lift-engineman of High Street Coatham, Robert Wray (32) a helper of Widgeon Street, married with four children; Edward Dooley (30) a furnace keeper of Coatham; Edwin Austin (40) a charger of Partridge Street, married with five children; Alfred Drinkwater (29) a furnace keeper of James Terrace married with four children; Charles Weatherill (36) a mine filler of Plover Street.

Warrenby from the bridge, 1921. Prominent is the Warrenby Hotel. The little boy on the right is Harry Bilton.

Above: The man on the right under the ring is Robert Pybus, stationmaster. The words above the windows read Warrenby Crossing and not Warrenby Halt, the name given to the crossing as employees used it as a dropping off point to go to work. Robert Pybus, who was resident somewhere in Warrenby at the time of his marriage in 1903, gave his occupation as 'railway signalman' on the certificate.

Opposite below: The Temke family home was 14 Warrenby Road. Mrs Temke had the adjoining property which was situated on the corner of Warrenby Road and Rocket Terrace which she ran as an overnight stay for travellers, as many were coming into the area to find work in the iron works. Amelia Temke is standing in the centre at the back, Carl Albert George is seated cross-legged, John is standing in the centre at the front, Melita is kneeling centre front, Billy is in his mother's arms and Helen in her father's arms.

William Alexander Nunn and Emily Pybus (daughter of Robert) married on 21 April 1903 at Christ Church in the parish of Coatham.

A family scene from around 1913. Maggie Ayton (*née* Buxton) with her children Ben (standing next to her), Jim (centre) Edith (right), Marie (front, next to her mother) and Alice (in front of Edith).

William and Sarah Webster of Warrenby.

Right: Albert and Minnie Want with their children − and pets − pose for the camera outside 39 Brands Terrace, Warrenby, *c.* 1900.

Below: Taken during the First World War, *c.* 1915. From left to right, seated: Albert Want with Cissie standing on his lap, Poppy, Jessie, Mrs Want with baby Minnie on her lap, Standing: Helen, Lilly, Mabel.

Above: Henry Mealing was a grocer on Tod Point Road. Here, around 1890, we see Grandma Crow, Ernest Mealing, Theodore Mealing, Mabel (standing in the doorway to right of the shop front) and the hen has the freedom of Tod Point Road.

Left: Elizabeth Caddy at the front of 37 Brands Terrace.

Above: The wedding of Mr Michael Murphy, a former Middlesbrough FC footballer, and his wife Alice.

Right: Margaret Beatrice Murphy, aged four years old, with her mother Alice Murphy (*née* Ranson) and her grandmother Catherine Murphy (*née* Moylan).

Two larger houses built for works management on Tod Point Road, they were situated between Teal Street and Coney Street.

Beatrice Johnson and Margery Close in Widgeon Street, possibly in the 1920s. The little girl in the centre has a tight reign on the horse.

The wedding group of Jack Robinson and
Sarah Jane Fox in the sunny backyard of
the Fox family home on Hicks Terrace,
1912.

William and Sarah Fox celebrate fifty years
of married life by posing for a picture on
their golden wedding anniversary in 1922.
Their marriage had taken place at Christ
Church, Coatham.

The army barracks, home of the Royal Artillery during the war years, and church, Warrenby.

Warrenby Steel Works canteen staff with the troops sharing hospitality during the Second World War. Included in the photograph are Florrie Wright, Miriam Phelps, Peggy Want and Jessie Want.

Above left: Alice Barker with her eldest grandson Billy Bage, *c.* 1930.

Above right: Morris Marshall Barker of Tod Point Road walking around Redcar in 1942.

Above: Marsh Farm, Warrenby. A listed building.

Left: Mr and Mrs Troup of Marsh Farm, in the 1940s.

Opposite below: Sacred Heart Church, Redcar, August 1937. From left to right, back row: Annie Leith, Edward Lloyd, groom Arthur Carling, bride Elizabeth (*née* Underhill), the groom's cousin Elizabeth Lorrains. Seated: Theresa Robson, Hugh Andrew Lloyd.

Above: The wedding group of Joe and Gertie Lloyd. The best man was Jim White and the bridesmaids were Lenora Lloyd (left) and Bertha Thornhill.

Brother and sister Billy and Alice Bage at the back of Paisley Barracks on Tod Point Road, *c.* 1934.

The three amigos in the back alley between Teal Street and Coney Street are, from left to right: Len Holmes, Billy Holmes and Colin Barker with his dog Rex. This photograph dates from around 1945.

Three generations of a family, *c.* 1958. From left to right: Audrey Lambert, Teresa O'Conner, David Lambert, with Kath Lambert holding brother Paul. In front, Linda Lambert.

Teresa O'Conner and Nellie Swan taking a break from their daily chores in their sunny backyard in Teal Street.

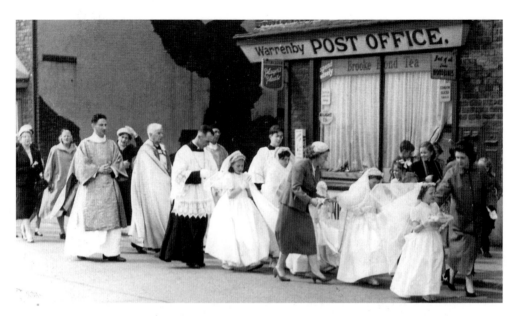

St Mary's procession passing the village post office, 1954.

Above: St Mary's May procession passing Hugh Bell cottages in 1957. Included in the picture at the front are the cushion-bearer Betty Barker, Monsignor Brunner, Father Beastey, Father O'Connell and Freda Lloyd.

Opposite above: Winnie Gibbon, on Warrenby sands, with her grandchildren, 1959. From left to right: Owen, Stephen, Tony, -?-.

Opposite below: Mrs English on the right, with company, *c.* 1950.

A gathering of friends at the Warrenby Hotel. From left to right: Alice Murphy, Doreen Grimwood, Mrs Rudd, Mick Murphy. In front: Jim Grimwood.

The No. 87 bus ran from Warrenby to New Marske hourly. Here we see the bus at the terminus near Marsh Farm in 1960. *(Courtesy of Philip Battersby)*

Above: A happy group are playing games in the back alley. From left to right, back row: Dorothy and Carole Thwaites, Dot Sexton, Barbara Thwaites, Patricia Sexton, George Thwaites, Colin Mead. Front row: Andrew and Christopher Dargen, Tommy Sexton, -?-, -?-, David ?

Right: Mrs Thornhill of Downey Street on the step with one of her many grandchildren.

Above: To mark her recent marriage to Harry Walker, Evelyn Walker (*née* Fox) received a stainless steel tea service from the employees at Redcar works in 1969. Presenting the gift is Mr R. Morrison, chairman of Redcar Works Joint Welfare Council. The others present are, from left to right: Harry Walker, V. Robins, M.D. Cummings (representative from the Ingot Bogie Shop), D Curtice.

Left: Evelyn Walker (*née* Fox) was a boot store attendant and completed twenty-nine years service at the works.

Above: Warrenby Gala Day, *c.* 1949. From left to right, back row: Sarah Barker, Mabel Wyman, the Mayor and Mayoress of Redcar, Annie Malone, Mrs Troup, Peggy Ditchburn, nurse Johnny O'Conner. Middle row: Pat Gilroy, Dorothy Briggs, Sandra Briggs, Gordon Webster. Front row: Ann and Mary Morris, John Wyman, Henry Gibbon.

Right: May Troup (centre) and friends enjoying the occasion.

Gala Day. From left to right, back row: Ronnie Boswell, Harry Tinsley, Bill Slightholme, Ethel Rowe, Jack Williams. Front row: Beryl Minowl, Minnie Noble, Elsie Granger, Nell Close, Alice Williams, Mrs McComick, *c.* 1950.

Annie Leith and Mick Gibbon at the Wild Duck Street VE Day party. They are impersonating Peter Brough and Archie Andrews, who were the stars of a popular radio program named *Educating Archie* in the 1940s.

Warrenby School, 1914.

From left to right, back row: Pat Arbon, Gillian Minowl, Pam Leonard, Jean Knight. Seated: Patricia Sexton, Linda Close, Jean Stainsby, Eileen Fitzgerald, Elsa Storey. The cup was won at sports day.

Warrenby people among the crowd at Ayrsome Park, Middlesbrough attending and listening to the Family Prayer Rally of Father Peyton, *c.* 1951. Father Peyton's slogan was 'The Family that Prays Together, Stays Together'. This emphasis may be why families often went as groups to hear him.

Alvina and Albert Marshall Ward. Albert who was born at 48 James Terrace, Warrenby on 9 February 1894 was secretary of the Dorman Long Warrenby Athletic Club for many years.

Right: Edwin Burdette was remembered for his well-kept garden, which could be viewed from Warrenby Bridge as it was situated along the side of the railway line. Edwin was groundsman at the local grammar school.

Below: From left to right: Charles Burdette, his wife Agnes, Sarah Jane Robinson, Liz Fox. This photograph was taken in 1952.

Left: Michael Knight was born in Warrenby in 1891. The Government released Michael from the Army in 1916 to help man the steel works because of a shortage of manpower. Michael and his wife Nora returned to Warrenby and lived in Wigeon Street.

Below: On Yer Bike! Betty Boswell, Mrs Whyman, Bertha Lettin and Joan Rowe, office cleaners from Warrenby Steel Works.

National Service lads say goodbye in 1952. Lenny Holmes (left) is leaving for Korea, centre is Tony Milburn, and Colin Barker (right) is off to Malaya..

Dave Lawson, Kenny Arbon and Jimmy Rudd in 1959. This photograph was taken on Redcar seafront while Jimmy was on leave from the RAF.

The Troup family plays alone in Plover Street in the 1970s; all the other children have left Warrenby. Ann, Elizabeth and May are watched by their mother Margaret and their sister Helen.

One of the last photographs of habitable Warrenby. The village was demolished during the 1970s, the residents re-housed and Warrenby became an area for light industry.

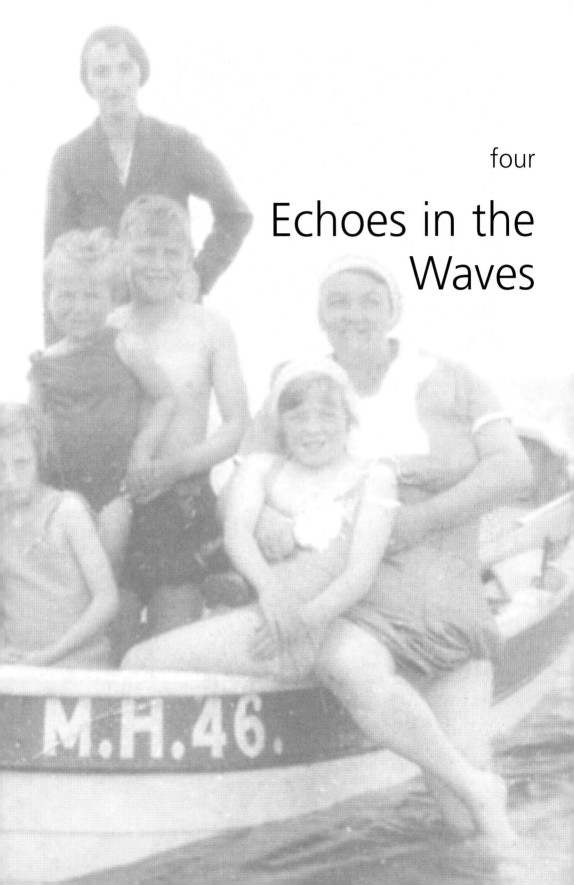

four

Echoes in the Waves

M.H. 46.

A photograph of a painting by William Woodhouse of Crathorne portrays fisherman James Thompson in 1888 aged fifty.

The oldest lifeboat in England, the *Zetland* on display at Leonard Cheshire Home, Marske by the Sea.

Dr George Young of the Teesmouth Lifeboat with coxswain Jim Thompson. Young Mark Thompson seems delighted to witness his uncle's safe return, *c.* 1939.

Holidaymakers at Redcar enjoy a pleasure trip in the *Pretoria* in 1935.

S.S. *Athina Lavanos* ashore at Redcar on 28 February 1937.

Opposite above: Johnny King (left) and Mark Thompson setting off early in the morning to take their gear to the boat.

Opposite below: Brothers Mark (left) and Jim Thompson (right).

Above: From left to right: the Vicar of St Peter's, Daisy Ellen Thompson, Admiral Oxley, Miss Oxley, Mr Oxley, Michael Thompson, Jack Thompson snr.

Above: The *Lady Maude* and crew, *c.* 1960. From left to right: Gordon Barry, Bruce Graham, Cyril Bryan, with their father Cyril Bryan Maude.

Right: Three generations celebrate The Queen's Silver Jubilee in 1977. From left to right: son John Emmerson, father James Emmerson, and grandson Michael Emmerson.

Opposite below: The christening party of the fishing vessel *Lady Oxley* being held at 6 South Terrace. From left to right, back row: Admiral Oxley's son, Jack Thompson snr, Daisy Ellen, the Vicar of St Peter's, Mark Thompson, Harry Tomlin, Jack Atkinson. Front row: Aunt Lil, Miss Oxley, Michael Thompson, Nellie Thompson with her nephew Arnold, June Storey, Nancy Storey, and Mr Pattison, who was proprietor of the Redcar High Street post office.

During the Christmas period around 1950 a whale was washed ashore at Redcar. Fishermen and early morning bus crews were first on the scene.

From left to right: –?–, Mark Thompson, the 'gaffer' Bert Bowers, Jim Thompson, Jack Thompson, –?–, –?–.

Above: Police sub-aqua diving team liaise with the Redcar sector.

Opposite below: While fishing off Marske Ron Sabison saw something splashing in the water; he found it to be a blue budgie thrashing about. After pulling it from the water in a very bedraggled state he wrapped it in a towel and took it home. An advert was placed in the *Evening Gazette* where a woman claimed it. The bird had escaped from an aviary in her garden.

Jim Thompson receiving his medal from coastguard officials in honour of twenty-five years' service.

A presentation ceremony by the Home Secretary on behalf of the Queen to present Ron Sabison with the British Empire Medal for services to Redcar Coastguards. The ceremony was held at the Old Wartime House of Lords. From left to right: Dorothy Sabison, Michael Howard, Ron Sabison BEM, Chief Coastguard Mr Derek Ancona. This was the last time the BEM was issued.

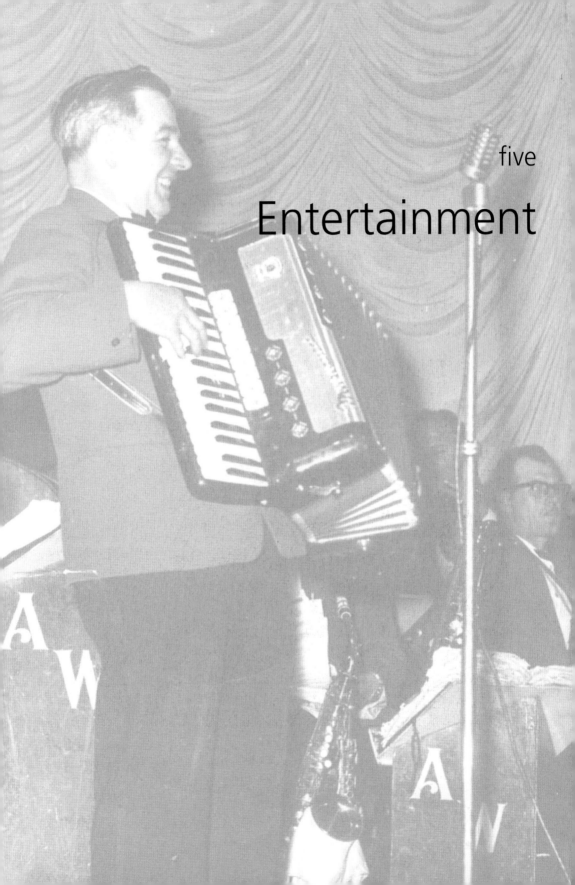

five

Entertainment

Redcar Pier Ballroom presents Danny Mitchell and his Hawaiian dancers in 1959.

Opposite above: The Danny Mitchell Orchestra in 1950.

Opposite below: A versatile female musician, Brenda Oliver, in 1950.

Popular vocalist Frank Jarrett at the Pier
Ballroom in 1950.

A record was key to success

A VOICE able to sing popular
melodies in the modern
idiom is one of the biggest box
office attractions in show
business today.

At Redcar there is such a voice,
but it is just beginning its climb
to the top.

It belongs to 32-year-old Frank
Jarrett, vocalist with Danny
Mitchell's resident band at the
Corporation-owned Pier Ballroom
for the past four years. Already
he has attracted B.B.C. sound
and television producers as well
as one of the country's leading
record making firms.

Just over six months ago Frank
sent a recording to the Man-
chester studios of the B.B.C. For
three months he heard nothing.

Left: The young Alan Gale.

Below: Alan Gale's Wavelets, 1948, with Alan (centre) in evening suit. Pictured bottom are Pat riding (Mrs Gale) and Ethel Formby (sister of George Formby).

Alan Waller was one of several band leaders who helped create the Big Band sound of the1940s and '50s. His orchestra was one of the area's most popular dance bands, along with Charles Amer and Danny Mitchell. Although each had their own venue, they were known to make guest appearances in each other's orchestras. Other local talented musicians would receive rapturous applause when announced as a surprise act.

THE COATHAM

HOTEL

REDCAR

★

Christmas Eve Dance

★ *In the Regency Ballroom* ★

MONDAY, 24th DECEMBER, 1984
DANCING TO THE
Alan Waller Orchestra

7-45—11-45p.m.   —   Tickets £1-50

Right: George Ireland makes a guest appearance with Alan Waller.

REDCAR SILVERWOOD BAND

presents...

New Year's Eve
Party Dance

★ *with Alan Waller* ✳

The Swan Hotel Ballroom
Redcar

8-15—12-15

BUFFET & BAR FACILITIES

By Invitation only £2.00

Left: A talented Redcar musician, Nicky Walker, who has played with many orchestras including Sid Lawrence, The Glen Miller Band UK, The Pasadena and several TV bands.

Below: On holiday in Perth, Western Australia, George Ireland was recognised and invited to play the Wurlitzer.

Above: Billy Scarrow's Optimists at an open-air concert on Redcar seafront, 1934.

Right: The Grand opening of the Majestic, Dormanstown.
(BUG + FLEA)

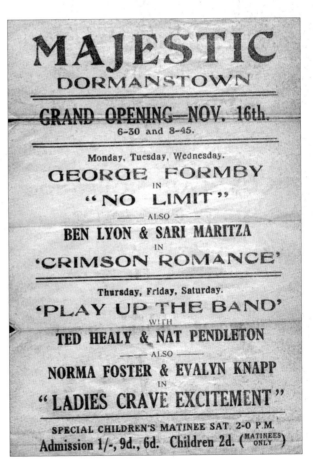

MAJESTIC
DORMANSTOWN

GRAND OPENING—NOV. 16th.
6-30 and 8-45.

Monday, Tuesday, Wednesday.

GEORGE FORMBY
IN
"NO LIMIT"
—— ALSO ——

BEN LYON & SARI MARITZA
IN
'CRIMSON ROMANCE'

Thursday, Friday, Saturday.

'PLAY UP THE BAND'
WITH
TED HEALY & NAT PENDLETON
—— ALSO ——
NORMA FOSTER & EVALYN KNAPP
IN
"LADIES CRAVE EXCITEMENT"

SPECIAL CHILDREN'S MATINEE SAT. 2-0 P.M.

Admission 1/-, 9d., 6d. Children 2d. (MATINEES ONLY)

Local Redcar band The Knight Riders.

Mrs Petch, a self-taught musician.

Above: Dancing the night away
at the Pier Ballroom. On the left
are Billy and Dot Thompson,
centre Arthur and Annie Gibbon,
with John and Edith Thompson
on the right, 1962.

Right: The Lynn and Walter
Rodgers School of Dancing
presentation evening, held in the
Queen's Hotel. Walter Rodgers is
in the centre, while the recipient
of the award is C.G. Barker.

The original Redcar Male Voice Choir formed in around 1930 during a time of mass unemployment. Members gather in Westbourne Grove, Redcar to travel by bus to Danby for an engagement in 1934. Known names are Ossie Gill, H. Robinson, Dorothy Foster, Fred Seaton, J.W. Richardson, R.H. Hunter, / ? Gard, ? Cox, ? Allison, ? Whiting, ? Armstrong, ? Knowles, Fordy Featherstone, H. Smithers, J. Phillips, Maltby brothers, Bill Robinson, ? Naylor, ? Leng, Ted Harrison.

Members of the Redcar Male Voice Choir. Included in the photograph are Ron Jefferson, John Weir, Ray Davis, Harry Coates, Vic Parnell, Dave Armstrong, Peter Whittaker, Martin McNulty, Jean Weir, Margaret Fick, Tom McCafferty and Keith Burn.

Dormanstown dance held in the band hut, 1950. From left to right, front row: Mr Lee, Mrs Postgate, Jean Jordon, Ann Johnson, Clive Howard, Mary Brockly, -?-, -?-, Edna Snowdon, -?-. Second row: Joan Hatton, Mervyn Thomas, -?-, Sheila Taylor, Eric Dales, Mrs Hutchinson, Miss Warne, -?-, Mrs Willard, -?-. Third row: Mr Lawrence, Mr Rogers, Mrs Theaker, Mrs Hall, Mr Hall, Mrs Godfrey, Mr Falconer, Mrs Falconer, Mr Johnson, Mrs Johnson, -?-, -?-, Mr Willard, -?-, -?-, Mrs Lee. Back row: Mrs Rogers, -?-, -?-, ? Allendon, Elizabeth Hatton, Mrs Warburton, Mrs Wilkinson, Alma Readman, Mrs Hutchinson, Mrs Lawrence, Mrs Warne, Jim Fawns, Miss Warne, Mr Warne.

Alan Waller's Silverwood Band taking a break near the Regent cinema.

Redcar Male Voice Choir took part in a spectacular event in 1991 where choirs from steelmaking areas came together to sing.

An afternoon entertaining the residents of the White House Nursing Home in Brotton. Ray Davis (left) and David Armstrong take a break from singing with a spot of comedy.

New Marske Silver Prize Band parading on West Terrace in 1955, lead by bandmaster Mr Kitching followed by Bernard Martin in the front row on his trombone.

The Redcar Works Silver Prize Band.

The Redcar Male Voice Choir members say goodbye to Pat Fox who had reformed the choir in the 1960s following a lapse. From left to right, back row: Jim Douglas, Billy Burnip, Ron Hutchinson, Dennis Clarke, Tim Leneghan. Third row: Len Brockely, Frank Lovat, Ron Robinson, Eric Yarker, Roy Readman, Tom McCafferty. Second row: Joe Dale, –?–, John Thompson, –?–, Keith Burns, –?–, Stan Ross. Front row: John McElvaney, Polly Elliot, Brian Wilson, Maurice Trousdale, Pat Fox, Jean Weir, Les Grant.

The Redcar Male Voice Choir entertain at the Ann Charlton Lodge, Redcar. Front row left is Jean Weir, with Andy Waugh and Ann Charlton.

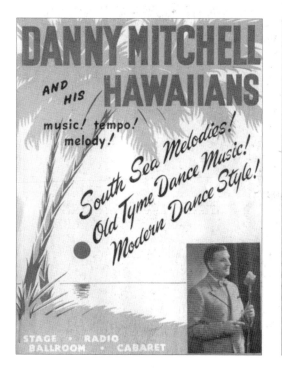

Entertainment by Redcar Male Voice Choir at Luke Senior Nursing Home, Guisborough. Standing are the manager of the home Julie Bentley and choir member Andy Waugh. Seated are the residents.

Other local titles published by Tempus

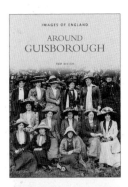

Around Guisborough
PAM WILSON

This collection of over 200 archive photographs portrays life in and around the town of Guisborough during the last 150 years. From snapshots of horse-drawn vehicles and charabancs, annual carnivals and motorbike gymkhanas, to vistas of children playing in fields which now house new generations of Gisborians, each picture reveals the gradual physical change in the buildings and streets, and offers a unique glimpse into Guisborough's past.
7524 3075 0

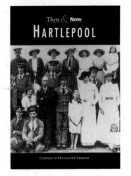

Hartlepool Then & Now
DOUGLAS R.P. FERRIDAY

This collection of over ninety-five pairs of images provides a nostalgic look back at the long history of the sea port of Hartlepool, from its social and industrial origins to the thriving commercial town it has become today. Intriguing comparisons are made between the businesses, streets, shops and local townsfolk, and each pair of pictures is accompanied by informative text charting the enormous development which has taken place over the last century.

0 7524 2660 5

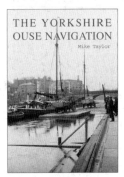

The Yorkshire Ouse Navigation
MIKE TAYLOR

The River Ouse has played a vital role in moving goods and people to and from York since Roman times. In this volume Mike Taylor has used an extensive resource of maps and photographs, dating from the late nineteenth century to the present, to illustrate the development of cargo-carrying on the river and its tributary rivers and canals. Images include vessels at work on the Navigation, boatbuilding as several Ouse sites, and the peril of the powerful tides
0 7524 2369 X

The Forgotten Landscapes of the Yorkshire Wolds
CHRIS FENTON-THOMAS

This book traces the development of the Yorkshire Wolds from 1000 BC to the present day. Sometimes the place was open pasture crossed by winding tracks and peppered with burial monuments, whilst at others it was occupied, farmed and enclosed by a network of boundaries. Chris Fenton-Thomas outlines the changes the Wolds went through and how these contrasted with the surrounding lowlands. He also shows how many aspects of this landscape survived over the centuries.
0 7524 3346 6

If you are interested in purchasing other books published by Tempus, or in case you have difficulty finding any Tempus books in your local bookshop, you can also place orders directly through our website

www.tempus-publishing.com